A gilded image of the Amida Buddha,
enshrined inside the Phoenix Hall of
Byodo-in in Uji, gazes to the west over
an earthly interpretation of his
celestial Pure Land.

A footbridge links the verdant moss slopes of Saiho-ji, Kyoto's famed "Moss Temple," which envelop its meandering pond.

IN THE
JAPANESE GARDEN

Photography by Michael S. Yamashita

Foreword by Shiro Nakane

Text by Elizabeth Bibb

Starwood Publishing, Inc.

Washington, D.C.

ISBN 0-912347-80-5
Printed in Japan by Dai Nippon Printing Ltd.

CONTENTS

The Japanese garden is an interpretation of the natural landscape as perceived by the Japanese in the cultural and social mirror of their times. While the types and combinations of plants within the garden reflect the surrounding indigenous vegetation, they, like society, change slightly from year to year.

Western visitors to Japanese gardens often comment that except for an occasional azalea or camellia, there are few flowering plants. Were these Westerners to visit the classical gardens of China, they might make the same observation. Despite a 1300-year-old tradition and so close an association with Japan that even most Japanese are convinced it is an entirely indigenous art form, almost all aspects of the Japanese garden originated in China.

Classical Chinese gardens were built primarily during the Ming and Ch'ing dynasties (1368–1912).

Though clearly different from Japanese gardens, they share a similar focus. Their most important design elements are *jiashau* (rockery) and manmade structures; trees and plants are secondary.

As Chinese culture spread throughout Japan, Japan's primeval evergreen forest was felled, and the Japanese garden started to echo the natural course of plant succession. When flowering plants took hold on newly cleared lands, they began to appear in gardens as well. Fields slowly reverted to forests again, and pine thickets inspired new designs. Today, with the increasing number of naturally occurring evergreens, Japanese are forgetting that flowering plants ever played a major role in their gardens.

Unlike other arts, that of the Japanese garden gives equal weight to beauty and utility. Gardens serve not only as objects for appreciation but also as environments for living. The Japanese garden, a local art with local origins, is becoming

popular throughout the world because its aesthetic addresses something which is universally human and therefore beyond race, nationality, or culture.

Isamu Noguchi and I. M. Pei are successful in the United States not because they build traditional Japanese gardens or Chinese structures here, but because, through expressing their Asian natures within an American context, they have created something entirely new.

Building a garden is like painting on a three-dimensional canvas. Rocks are one of the most important elements. They are arranged according to the laws of perspective, in well-balanced compositions based upon the triangle. But the master Japanese gardener learns his craft through natural observation, not theoretical study. As in a painting, literalism and abstraction play a part in the Japanese garden; we judge each in terms of both composition and technique.

Straw covers blanket these subtropical cycads against winter storms at the garden of Kyoto's Jonan-gu, designed by Kinsaku Nakane.

Westerners often admire the pine trees in Japanese gardens. But though they can read about the time-consuming and highly painstaking care these trees require, and can eventually come to understand the relationship between the trees and garden, when Westerners start to think about building their own Japanese gardens, they just remember the beautifully shaped pines. They forget first the difficulty of maintenance, second the difference in climate, and third the fact that few Westerners have cultivated the degree of patience characteristic of the Japanese. I am often reminded of cheerleaders' pompons when I see shaped pines in Japanese gardens in the United States and Europe. Pine trees, stone lanterns, and washbasins no more make up the essence of the Japanese garden than chrysanthemums, Mount Fuji, and geisha girls represent Japanese culture.

My friend Mike Yamashita traveled throughout Japan taking photographs which capture the essential beauty of the Japanese garden. I hope that along with Elizabeth Bibb's text, they will give you the kind of enlightened appreciation of the Japanese garden that will enable you to incorporate its elements into your own garden designs, creating something, like the best of the Japanese gardens, which springs from your unique sense of the natural world.

11

A solitary stone holding a universe in its craggy facets. A sweeping sea of sand deep within a cryptomeria grove. A Zen monk deliberately, slowly raking fine gravel into swirling whirlpools. A single maple leaf suspended on a glistening bed of moss. An expansive panorama of sky and trees reflected in a pond dotted with miniature islands. Distant mountains framed by the panes of translucent shoji. Stones, plants, water, sand and gravel, and space—all are elements intrinsic to Japanese gardens and, in essence, gardens in themselves.

Often best appreciated as the sum of their elements, Japanese gardens are defined by details, none of which is random or accidental, however abstract or whimsical it may seem. By observing the garden through its composite parts, we see into its soul.

To the Western mind, a garden is a straightforward, albeit often inspiring, place. It is where flowers, herbs, vegetables, or trees are

cultivated, where nature is harnessed and redesigned. But to the Japanese, a garden is not so much a place in which to control or mingle with nature, as a place for contemplation and for transcending the bounds of nature. Japanese gardens, even those that compare in size to Western-style parks, have an intimacy, a unity, and a kinship with nature that extend back to the roots of Japanese culture and religion.

The story of Japanese gardens spans thousands of years; gardening styles have evolved as Japanese society has, through isolation and commerce. It is a story that actually begins with the very origins of the Japanese people.

In their transition from a nomadic culture that survived by hunting and fishing to an agrarian society, the Japanese became wedded to the land for their sustenance. Even though their livelihoods were subject to the whims of nature, the early Japanese did not perceive natural forces as hostile. Rather, these forces

were believed to be divine spirits *(kami)* who could manifest themselves in all natural things: mountains, trees, stones.

The *kami*, who were at once beneficent and brutal, were believed responsive to man. As a plentiful harvest was the primary goal of these ancient farmers, much effort was made to entice the *kami* to grace the earth with their presence,

bringing good fortune with them. This was the origin of Shinto, the native animistic religion of Japan.

To draw the *kami* to earth, clearings were made in forest groves, spread with white sand, and purified so that they would be ready to receive the gods. Marked only with a rice-fiber rope, the clearings (*niwa*) became the earliest shrines. In defining the perimeters of a small portion of the natural world, the Japanese created their first gardens, not for the pleasure of man, but for the gods. The word *niwa* still means garden.

To honor the sun goddess Amaterasu, without whose life-giving light man could not survive (and from whom the Japanese imperial line was believed to have descended), a huge shrine was consecrated at Ise in 260 B.C. Upon entering Ise, one of the most sacred spots in Japan, time seems irrelevant. The towering, ageless cryptomeria trees are alive with the spirits in the early morning before the tour buses arrive. The sounds—water rushing over stones, the clip-clop of a priest's black-lacquered clogs, the gravel crunching beneath the visitor's feet—add an extra dimension to the experience of the shrine.

Gardens such as Ritsurin-en in Takamatsu, a daimyo stroll garden of 7,590,000 square feet including artificial hills and ponds, are a celebration of nature.

Though the atmosphere at Ise's inner shrine is thick with sacred and regal undertones, the space is surprisingly unadorned. It consists of two sections. One, an idealized version of an early grain storehouse, is the building which houses sacred relics. It is counterbalanced by the second section, a white expanse of gravel hidden from view beyond four layers of fencing. Where some would see an empty space, others sense sanctified ground for summoning the gods. This holiest of shrines is in essence no different from the first *niwa* cleared in the forest to beckon the *kami*.

Every twenty years the wooden structure is dismantled and rebuilt on the other side of the partition as part of an ancient purification ritual. All that remains of the original structure is a sacred pillar standing starkly alone in the midst of the gravel. This practice has continued, with almost no interruptions, since 690 A.D.

Ise illustrates, in many ways, the starting point from which primitive Japanese animism evolved into a garden aesthetic. Ise is a Japanese garden in its starkest—and purest—sense. To see the shrine is to feel it. The senses are alerted that here in this forest the gods do indeed gather. The woods and the river are vibrant and animated, yet strangely still. Here there is splendor in simplicity, spirituality without icons, art without adornment.

And so, the Japanese garden has evolved from the eerily abstract and surprisingly modern sacred clearings to the elaborately executed miniature universes of Japan's classical era and on to the minimalist constructions of the twentieth century. Along the way, a finely tuned tradition of garden building has been cultivated into an intricate choreography of design, texture, shape, and sound.

Although at times the Japanese have embellished their gardens with almost rococo lavishness, they nevertheless return to basics for inspiration. With its vast sweep of gravel, Ise became the prototype for the traditional Shinto shrine and, in time, for the imperial residences. The emperor's home was also a shrine, a site for the conduct of both secular and nonsecular affairs. The great gravel tracts became the courtyards of the imperial palaces (*yuniwa*), where nobles gathered to pay homage to the emperor and great events were staged.

The imperial court first promoted and refined the tradition of garden design, gradually adding to the austere gravel spaces the elements that have come to be so closely identified with Japanese gardens: stones, water, and various flora. Once you slow down to appreciate these elements—and Japanese gardens are constructed to ensure that you do—it is possible to begin to sense the presence and power of natural forces, just as the early Shinto followers must have done 1,700 years ago.

As the Shinto tradition grew

stronger and more ritualized, other influences gained ground in Japan. The Japanese began to look beyond their island nation to the west and north and coupled their beliefs, based in Shinto precepts, with creative borrowing from the highly refined societies of China and Korea.

Chinese influences exerted a powerful force on the island nation. The active commerce between China and Japan when Nara was the seat of the island kingdom's imperial government gave the Japanese an acute awareness of their perimeters. The lengthy boat crossings to the mainland familiarized the Japanese with their own windswept shores and inspired them to recreate these vistas at their royal courts.

In 607, Ono No Imoku, the leader of the first Japanese diplomatic mission to China, observed the ways in which the Chinese constructed elaborate and seemingly natural wonders—lakes, islands, moun-

tains—all in defined tracts of land. Ono returned to Nara with these landscaping lessons in mind, and his reports of Chinese gardening methods inspired the Japanese, who had already developed the skills necessary to execute the designs. They were adept at water handling, thanks to their experience with irrigation for rice cultivation; they were also accomplished at earth moving, having built elaborate earthen burial mounds surrounding the Nara plains during the Kofun period (300–ca. 700 A.D.).

Japan was fertile ground for a craftsman like Michiko no Takumi when he arrived from Korea in 612.

Michiko is credited with constructing one of the first documented garden designs in Japan. He was known by the name "The Ugly Artisan" and was initially ridiculed for his white, blotchy skin. But his appearance belied his abilities as a gardener.

Michiko crafted for the Empress Suiko a garden that was inspired by Mount Sumeru, the mythical sacred mountain referred to in Buddhist teachings. Complete with an artificial lake and island, Michiko's garden clearly exhibited his design skills. Despite the dearth of relics from that time, there is evidence that

The shoden (sacred hall) of Ise's inner shrine, hidden behind four layers of fencing, looms over the gravel courtyard of the hall's alternate site.

(Facing) The sound of a Shinto priest's lacquered clogs breaks the silence on a path leading from the inner shrine at Ise on the Shima Peninsula.

At Daisen-in in Kyoto, rocks and gravel create a waterfall and river inspired by a Sung landscape painting.

the empress' garden started a trend; remains have been found of a garden built in the lake-hill-island motif by her uncle, Soga no Umako, in 620.

So intrinsic did this style of garden become to Japanese landscaping that the word *shima* (island) was used to designate gardens until around the eighth century. Although the name has changed, this motif remains one of the basic forms of Japanese gardens.

As Japanese gardeners honed their skills, stones eventually were added to the islands to represent the looming mountains of the Chinese landscape. Stones came to represent not just mountain peaks, but also cascades, rivers, and seas. The Japanese incorporated their abilities in water handling and stone setting into channeling water along meandering manmade streams that fed into ponds. They also began to employ representational techniques

to imply streams and rivers: raked white sand and pebbles indicated flowing waters, deeply creviced boulders became dynamic waterfalls, and rugged stones recalled windswept shorelines weathered by the wind, the sea, and the years.

The imported arts of China's T'ang dynasty thrived in Japan during the Nara period. Things Chinese, from landscape design, architecture, and law to city planning, were the vogue. Nara, and later Kyoto, were laid out according to the Chinese urban grid model. The geomantic laws of *feng shui*, the art of harmonious placement, were also introduced to the Japanese, providing a basis for the most advantageous siting of cities, homes, fields, and gardens.

But the influx of foreign ideas did not supplant native ones. Though they absorbed the cultural and religious tenets of China, including Buddhism, Taoism, Confucianism, and even the ancient art of

geomancy, the Japanese retained nature as the ultimate reference point. Their gardens, even those most blatantly Chinese in style, illustrate this. Chinese Buddhist philosophy and its attendant cultural advancements coexisted and even mingled with and absorbed the native Shinto practices, rather than replacing them. Eventually, the *kami*, the natural deities, were accepted as manifestations of the Buddha, and temple districts often incorporated "guardian" Shinto shrines into their layout.

Along with the flourishing of native and imported culture, major shifts were occurring in the developing country. In 794, the capital was moved to Heian (now Kyoto), which translated means the "City of Peace and Tranquility." The period known by the same name is considered Japan's classical age (794–1185), and events of those times were pivotal to garden design. Kyoto—surrounded by mountains,

forests, ponds, lakes, and natural springs; influenced by Buddhism and the blossoming of Japan's own cultural arts; and presided over by the powerful imperial court—soon became the cradle of the Japanese garden.

A distinctive form of architecture

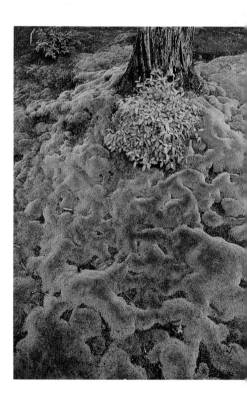

Over the centuries, Saiho-ji at times fell into disrepair, allowing moss to proliferate. Upon restoration, the moss remains as a predominate and identifying characteristic.

known as *shinden* (sleeping quarters) defined this period. It was a fusion of the formal Chinese building style and the more natural, less ornamental Japanese design as characterized by the sacred hall at Ise.

Gardens, too, thrived during this period and became refined as a courtly art fit for the emperor. Gardens were incorporated into the Imperial Palace and the *shinden*-style residences of court nobles. Although no physical remains of these grand gardens are left today, their place in the lives of the nobles is vividly recounted in *The Tale of Genji*, written by a noblewoman of the Fujiwara clan, Lady Murasaki, sometime around the year 1000.

Shinden structures were marked by a central hall surrounded by a number of subsidiary structures and linked by wooden walkways. Gardens, ranging from the austere courtyards reminiscent of shrine layouts in front of the imperial

residences, to intimate gardens called *tsubo* designed to fit in the spaces tucked beside the corridors linking the halls, to lavish pond and island gardens viewed from the veranda of the main hall, were adapted to this architectural form. Other buildings—the fishing and spring pavilions—were built alongside the pond on stilts. The nobility would pass Kyoto's hot, humid summer days and evenings in these pavilions, refreshed by the cool water beneath them and lulled by its sound. During the Heian period, gardens were designed for the pleasure and relaxation of the nobles who built them.

In 894, the imperial court ordered an end to the lively commerce between Japan and China. For nearly 300 years, the many ideas and philosophies that had been imported and imitated were allowed to ferment and acquire a uniquely Japanese flavor.

In the late Heian period, garden designers, who were most often

Buddhist priests but occasionally nobles, began to take note of the scenery beyond the garden's confines. Far-off trees and mountains were incorporated into the overall picture, adding to the depth and intensity of the garden. The technique, called "borrowed scenery," has continued to be used in garden planning.

At this time, Esoteric Buddhism reached the zenith of its popularity in Japan. The mysticism and exclusivity of this sect, which stressed that an understanding of complex teachings, chants, and meditation were the way to achieve enlightenment, was attractive to the nobility, who had access to learned scholars and time to study complicated sutras. Many Esoteric temples with gardens were built suitably high away from everyday life on mountaintops, which as in Shinto are considered sacred. But in the latter part of the Heian period, during the reign of the Fujiwaras, a military clan that supplanted the

power of the imperial family, the predominance of the Amidist sect brought Buddhism down from the mountaintops and made it accessible to commoners and nobles alike.

Amidism was founded in 1175 by the monk Honen, who had studied in China. Its teachings instructed that a single, pure act of faith was enough to guarantee admittance to

Buddha's mythical paradise, known as Jodo (Pure Land). Amidism hinged on belief in Amida, who, like Christ, deferred his godliness in order to save the faithful. As interest in Amidism mounted—and as the political climate grew increasingly unsettled—the aristocracy began constructing gardens that were recreations of Jodo as depicted in Chinese Amidist mandalas. These

were attempts at building, quite literally, heaven on earth.

The intricate mandalas depicted a beatific Amida Buddha facing a heavenly pond embellished with Buddhist symbols. The so-called Jodo gardens expanded on the already popular, and familiar, lake-island theme. The Phoenix Hall of Byodo-in in Uji, near Kyoto, is the best-preserved example of a Jodo

garden. In the middle hall of a *shinden*-style temple, flanked by two ornamental pavilions, Amida has sat serenely contemplating his Western paradise—a pond garden surrounded by willows and wisteria—for hundreds of years.

By the end of the Heian period, the tenets of gardening had become formalized and were compiled in a

*The two-legged **kotoji-gata**, so named because of its resemblance to a Japanese harp, has one foot in the pond and the other on an islet at Kenroku-en in Kanazawa.*

At Daichi-ji near Kyoto, guests can sample tea cakes while savoring the undulating azalea hedge that is the garden.

manual, the *Sakuteiki*. It is believed to have been written by a noble of the court, Tachibana no Toshitsuna (1028–1094). The book, the earliest known treatise on gardening, is filled with carefully delineated formulas for stone laying, stream placement, and planting.

Sakuteiki also includes strict proscriptions against certain practices. These stem from geomantic taboos based on *feng shui*, the Chinese art of harmonious

placement by maximizing the positive flow of energy and eliminating the negative flow of energy into a site. This energy is represented by good and evil spirits, embodied by fabulous dragons and tigers. A site out of balance can bode badly. For instance, garden builders were instructed not to move a stone that has been laid horizontally to a vertical position, because it would be cursed by "revengeful spirits." Likewise, illness was believed to result if a stone was laid too close to

the southwest pillar of a house.

Sakuteiki is a compilation of design techniques, superstitions, and religious beliefs. It is also a vivid record of the times. The tenets set forth in this book have remained a source for the basics of garden design through the modern day.

Even as gardens became more rigidly defined, the Japanese found ways to circumvent even the most stringent of taboos. Observance of the taboos, so the author of *Sakuteiki* seems to imply, should be followed only so long as creativity and inspiration were not stifled. While *feng shui* might call for placement of a stream to the east of a house, a Japanese gardener could always find a solution if the natural landscape made this impossible. Both *feng shui* and *Sakuteiki* suggest "cures" that compensate for unfavorable conditions. While a gardener might try to reroute the stream, he might also plant nine weeping willows as an antidote to any bad fortune. This resourcefulness, this determination not to be daunted by the elements, still marks the Japanese character.

In the *Sakuteiki*, the elements that have come to be considered the classical components of a Japanese garden were outlined. And each element—be it stone, water, trees, shrubs, gravel, sand, or even sound and space—was believed to have its own essence, its own "mind." This is expressed in the words *kowan ni shigatsu*, which mean "following the request of the stone." It was the garden builder's job to listen, to feel, and to respect that essence.

The overthrow of the Taira clan of military regents by the Minamoto clan marked the advent of the Kamakura period (1185–1333), so named because Minamoto no Yoritomo moved the seat of military and political power to Kamakura in 1180. This period saw the rise of the samurai warrior class, who embraced Zen Buddhism, the sect that stressed discipline, austerity,

meditation, and a denial of the self in pursuit of enlightenment. Warriors honed not only the arts of war (*bu*), but also the gentler arts of scholarship, literature, and the fine arts (*bun*). During this period, the first tea was imported from China. It is believed that in 1191, the Buddhist priest Eisai introduced the tea ceremony. The ritualized drinking of tea originated as an aid in staying alert during long hours of meditation.

Zen, with its stress on simplicity, humility, and purity, was a response to the overwrought court rituals and mysterious teachings of the Esoteric sect. Because it emphasized finding the path to Buddhahood through the menial, the ordinary, and the small, Zen also became a repository for a highly refined level of taste. Zen priests became accomplished painters, calligraphers, and sculptors, as well as gardeners, and thrived under the patronage of

powerful samurai, feudal lords, and even the shogun himself.

The Zen priest Muso Soseki, also known for his skills as a landscape designer, persuaded the Ashikaga shogun Takauji to resume trade with China, in part to fund a major garden project at Tenryu-ji in Kyoto. Priests like Muso Soseki, with their familiarity with the language and customs of China, became increasingly influential—and affluent—as a result of this trade. They became curators of culture, and their temples were the bases for a particularly vibrant artistic blossoming during this period.

Concurrent with the rise of Zen's influence was the development of the Sung school of painting in China. The monochromatic landscapes depicting sacred Buddhist mountains, waterfalls, lakes, and seas proved as inspirational as T'ang art had been centuries earlier. During the late

Kamakura period and into the Muromachi period, when political power was restored to Kyoto by Shogun Takauji in 1338, landscape painting and garden design became closely linked.

Muso was one of the first to bring aspects of Chinese Sung culture into garden design. The massive cliffs towering over the landscapes in Sung paintings complemented the Zen philosophy of humility in the face of the transitory nature of existence. These monochromes easily lent themselves to translation into the medium of stone. Muso carried the themes of the Sung school, even to the point of crafting literal representations of actual paintings, into his landscapes.

Muso is also credited with being the first to consider the garden as a medium for meditation. Two of the most famous gardens attributed to or influenced by him were actually constructed on the grounds of earlier gardens—the Kyoto gardens of Saiho-ji and Tenryu-ji. Building on their existing themes, Muso imbued them with the aesthetics of Zen philosophy.

At first sight, Saiho-ji (ca. 1339), also known as Kokedera (the Moss Temple), seems a distant cousin of the stark rock and gravel of later Zen

Perched on a rock at Kyoto's Ryoan-ji, a Buddhist monk is intent upon meticulously raking the fine gravel sea that swirls around him.

meditation gardens. Saiho-ji is lushly planted, with over 100 varieties of moss that have carpeted the garden floor over centuries. Its pond and islands are a reminder that it was originally an Amidist paradise garden.

But Muso added another dimension to Saiho-ji, making the garden a bridge between the pleasure gardens of the Heian period and a calmer, more contemplative garden style. In the upper level of the garden, above the pond, he built a composition entirely of

rocks that has the appearance of a powerful waterfall. They seem a natural outcropping of the landscape, although each one was carefully placed to ensure the optimum effect. This arrangement is one of the most dramatic examples of the dry-landscape technique (*karesansui*) that evolved into the meditation garden.

During the Muromachi period (1338–1573), when the shogunate ruled in Kyoto and the imperial family reigned in the mountains of Yoshino, eclecticism became more apparent in garden design. Although the country was politically divided, it was nevertheless a time of fusion of diverse elements. The vitality of the warrior classes was tempered by the refinement of Kyoto. Also during this period, Christian missionaries and Portuguese traders began importing the ways of the West. The period was distinguished by massive building projects that paid close attention to artistic detail.

This can be seen in Tenryu-ji, which marks a shift from earlier naturalistic representations of landscapes to more artistic and symbolic recreations of actual scenes. At Tenryu-ji, Muso incorporated elements of the dry-landscape motif into a garden that had originally been built in the *shinden* style. The vertical stones rising in the rear of the pond at Tenryu-ji echo not only Buddhist teachings but also Chinese mythology. And the Dragon's Gate waterfall—with a symbolic carp stone at its base—is a reference to the cascade on China's Yellow River where a legendary carp swam up the falls and was transformed into a dragon.

A shift in the scale of gardens became evident during this period. Gardens became smaller, more contained. The garden was becoming not only a representation of a landscape in miniature, but a microcosm of the entire universe. Stone groupings, too, began to take

*The care and tending of Saiho-ji
involves constant vigilance. Here, a
gardener gently sweeps maple leaves
from the lush carpet of moss.*

on new symbolism. In addition to the waterfall-carp motif, stones were placed in pairs, one vertical and one horizontal, echoing the tortoise and crane legend of Chinese mythology. The triad motif was also popular, representing the union of heaven, earth, and man or a triad of Buddhist deities.

Stone landscape groupings also acquired more suggestive qualities that left the meaning of a garden dependent upon the perception of the viewer. The famous garden at Daisen-in (1509) in the Kyoto temple complex of Daitoku-ji is a clear depiction of a Sung monochrome, with waterfall, boat, sea, and islands represented by stones and white sand. But it is also open to a number of interpretations. The literal translation is there, but the viewer can find hints to stir the imagination into finding other levels of meaning. A familiarity with the source of the inspiration for the garden enhances, but is not essential to, its appreciation.

On the other hand, the garden at Kyoto's Ryoan-ji, a Zen temple constructed just before Daisen-in, is the Japanese garden reduced to its most elemental state. With three abstract groupings of fifteen stones, it is revolutionary in its extremes. Although Ryoan-ji contains references to many sources, it is in no way a literal interpretation of any of them. The imagination, then, can fill in the answers to the questions left by these cryptic rocks.

While the placement of the garden's stones in a sea of sand is inarguably artistic, its primary function is to aid the observer in channeling meditative thoughts. The garden was originally devoid of vegetation and designed to be viewed from the wooden veranda of the temple; its borders are limited to a rectangular enclosure. Over the centuries, moss has added subtle shadings to the rocks, creating the patina of age known as *sabi*. Even though observers are not invited to walk into the garden, the wings of the mind can, with proper concentration, carry the viewer into the space.

Before gardens took such a radical turn in the form of ones like Ryoan-ji, there were foreshadowings of the influence that Zen would have on landscape design. The third Ashikaga shogun, Yoshimitsu, was a leader in garden building. He erected Kinkaku-ji—with its well-known Golden Pavilion, considered one of the finest estate gardens in Japan—at his retirement villa in 1397. Adding to the grounds that were originally designed in the *shinden* style, Yoshimitsu incorporated an eclectic mix at Kinkaku-ji. Influenced by Zen, yet appreciative of Amidist beliefs, and a patron of the arts, Yoshimitsu brought all these aspects to bear in his gardens.

The Golden Pavilion, the three-storied structure that housed both reception halls and a Jodo temple, extends into a pond set with rock formations. A serpentine shoreline creates an illusion of a much larger lake. The garden's dimensions—from the small-scale rock groupings in the immediate pond area to the massive, far-off mountainsides—add to the illusion of a more expansive space.

The effects of passing time and the changing of the seasons are powerfully felt at Kinkaku-ji, which after Yoshimitsu's death was converted to a Zen temple, as was his wish. The pond, the rocks, and the foliage around them are equally inspiring, whether swathed in snow or dotted with blazing reds and oranges during the autumn or lush in the greenery of the rainy spring and the humid summer. This all-season, or rather seasonlessness, interest is one of the characteristics of the Japanese garden that diverges from the Western notions of gardening.

Yoshimitsu's grandson, Yoshimasa, while not as effective a

The gleam of the Golden Pavilion at Kinkaku-ji in Kyoto—the focal point of the temple garden—contrasts with the intense greens of a Japanese maple.

The path led guests through a succession of detailed views—from a formal entrance to a series of twists and turns past a washbasin and lantern to a path of stepping stones—en route to the tea hut, a rustic, thatch-roofed structure. Stepping stones, bridges, and turns were intentionally included to slow guests down, to encourage them to leave worldly concerns at the garden gate. The garden, then, while entirely pleasant and enjoyable, was also completely functional.

A stone washbasin, lit in the evening by the light of a carved stone lantern, reminds guests that they must wash their hands and their mouths in order to come to the ceremony pure of thought, word,

leader as his grandfather, nevertheless followed his patronage of the arts. His noted gardens at Ginkaku-ji, with its Silver Pavilion (1483), became a center for the cultural pursuits of the day. Many traditional garden motifs are represented here, including hedge-lined walkways that direct the eyes to particular views and a lush hill-and-pond section with bridges and rock formations. The Zen aesthetic is most evident at Ginkaku-ji in a stark, dry garden of sand marked by a flat-topped cone reminiscent of the

sacred mountain, Fuji. A raised bed of sand raked into wavelike patterns surrounds the cone.

Yoshimasa also fostered the art of the tea ceremony, and the garden's Dojin-sai is believed to be the model for the traditional tea hut. Built as an accompaniment to the *wabi* tea ceremony promoted by the noted tea master and Zen monk, Shuko Murata (1423–1502), it is a departure from earlier, more elaborate tea houses. Instead of

grandiosity, the tea hut emphasizes rustic simplicity. Shuko performed his version of the tea ceremony here, placing great emphasis on humility.

A deceptively simple style of tea garden, the *roji* was inspired by Shuko's philosophy and was further refined by Sen no Rikyu (1520–1591), who recorded the essentials of the ritual in his treatise entitled *Sado* (*The Way of Tea*). In the *wabi* tea ceremony, the approach became an essential part of the entire ritual.

25

and deed. A tiny opening through which they must crawl into the actual tea room accentuates the egalitarian humbling that is necessary to enhance the simplicity of the tea ceremony. To enter the tea garden is to remove oneself from the world beyond, focus on the immediate, appreciate the smallest details of life, and remind oneself of the essentials. To the Zen mind, all else is illusion.

The tea garden relied on motion to be fully appreciated. These were not gardens meant to be viewed from the veranda of a temple or contemplated from afar. As with most Japanese gardens, no element in a *roji* is left to chance. A path is sprinkled with water, even if the skies are dry, to bring out the full depth and dimension of stones and moss. A lone maple leaf is intentionally left alongside a washbasin to remind visitors of the cycle of life and death.

The simple *roji* espoused by Shuko and Sen no Rikyu expanded into the more elaborate *sukiya* tea arbors built during the flamboyant Momoyama period (1573–1603) and Edo period (1603–1868). But even before these grand, parklike gardens were constructed, the expansive and enigmatic Momoyama leader, Toyotomi Hideyoshi, was at work on reconstructing his extravagant twelfth-century temple Sambo-in (1598), so that he might enjoy the gorgeous cherry blossoms for which its surrounding area is noted. Toyotomi, known for reunifying Japan and stratifying the classes, ordered a garden that was on a par with the opulence of the gilded art of his day. Although walking through the almost baroque garden discloses

much fascinating detail, it was designed to be viewed from the porches of the surrounding halls as well.

Over eight hundred stones were acquired and placed in the garden, including one—the Fujito stone—that was considered the most valuable rock in Japan. It was transported in silk wrappings with the care reserved for the most precious of art works. This same reverence for rare stones is seen today; stones chosen for use in gardens sometimes command thousands of dollars.

Following the Momoyama period, which had been the pinnacle of the samurai ethos, Japan entered into a rarefied state under the Tokugawa shogunate. From 1636 until 1853, when Commodore Matthew Perry arrived at Uraga, the country was closed to outside influences.

The political repression of the Tokugawa rulers might have been expected to exert a stultifying effect on the creative arts. Instead, ideas were allowed to ferment in an exclusively Japanese environment, undisturbed by the wars that had marked the earlier periods, as the Tokugawas' iron hand enforced peace. During this period, landscaping and architecture showed a nostalgia for the classical Heian age. The feudal lords (*daimyo*) incorporated *shinden* designs and Jodo and Zen concepts in their gardens. The scale of gardens grew during this period, as the *daimyo* flaunted their wealth even while their power was diminishing. Their large estate gardens, like Kenroku-en in Kanazawa, Koraku-en in Okayama, and Ritsurin-en in Takamatsu, began to take on the characteristics of Western-style parks.

The Edo period saw a shift in social class balance. The noble samurai, without wars in which to ply their skills, were reduced to the roles of civil servants. The *daimyo*, who had ruled over their fiefdoms with relative autonomy, were continually under the suspicion of the shogunate. As a means of reducing their power and influence as well as their fortunes, and to keep a watchful eye on the ever-ambitious and contentious lords, the shogun required them to maintain a residence in Edo (modern Tokyo) and live there for periods of time.

Garden designers have adopted Mount Fuji's nearly perfect conical shape (below) as an archetype, as in this stylized recreation at Ginkaku-ji in Kyoto (left).

Because the *daimyo* desired grand gardens to flaunt their wealth and holdings, they hired gardeners who had taken over the role once filled by the nobility and Buddhist priests and monks. Like many other tradesmen, gardeners had unified into trade guilds. With the advent of garden professionals, the earlier philosophical and artistic aspirations of garden design gave way to a more craftsmanlike approach. Garden building became a business rather than a form of individual expression, and gardens were increasingly defined by their classifications: hill-and-pond or flat; formal, semiformal, or informal; meditation, stroll, or tea.

Even though the Edo era did not see the bursts of creative artistry that so typified earlier periods, new and untried forms were still developing. Inspired by the Muromachi *roji*, which incorporated prescribed movement into the garden, Kobori

Enshu (1579–1647), a *daimyo* himself, is credited with creating what is known as the stroll garden. Here the visitor's route is prescribed, as in the tea garden, but the scale is enlarged. The direction of the path leads the eye not to minute details but to broad vistas and panoramic views of ponds, trees, flowers, bridges, and distant scenery.

Kenroku-en in Kanazawa represents the Edo-period *daimyo* estate garden at its height. This stroll garden, among the largest of its kind, was begun in 1676 and finished in 1837. Kenroku-en brought to bear all the elements accrued from a thousand years of garden design: shallow streams of transparent water trickling over a bed of carefully placed pebbles; shimmering ponds surrounded by ancient pines, their boughs suspended over the water, supported by wooden crutches; stone lanterns standing sentry at lakeside; and a tea house nestled near the

foot of a cascading waterfall.

Concurrently, the Edo period saw the rise of the merchant class. Without political clout or aristocratic trappings, the merchants nevertheless grew wealthy during Japan's isolation. As their ranks grew, they too began to want gardens as a sign of their prosperity. But without the huge tracts of land that the *daimyo* had at their disposal, the rising middle class turned back to miniaturization. The art of landscaping in miniature became accessible to the commoner during this period. Just as a feudal lord might have ordered a miniature Fuji to be constructed in his garden, as did Hosokawa Tadatoshi in Suizen-ji, the merchant class brought entire forests into their homes through bonsai, the art of dwarfing and shaping trees to grow in earthenware pots, and *bonkei*, or tray gardening. They also reintroduced *tsubo*-inspired gardens that fit into small passageways or spaces between their homes or businesses.

Once trade resumed with the rest of the world and the shogunate's reign was ended with the Meiji restoration of the imperial government, Japan again became a sponge for foreign ideas. The importation of Western notions of landscaping saw the establishment of public parks, like Ueno, Shinjuku, and Hibiya in Tokyo. But even as Western influences began to leave their imprint on Japanese culture, an intense devotion to traditions remained. The years as a closed society had crystallized the culture, making much of it impervious to change.

While each cultural period in Japan has had its own unique styles, the same elements have been repeatedly reinterpreted over time, so that today gardens are an amalgam of ancient and modern design. Stone, gravel, sand, water, plants—and their interplay with elements like space and sound—are still celebrated, regardless of how a garden is classified. The identical elements used by shogun and samurai, Buddhist monk and Shinto priest, Heian noble and Edo merchant alike are still a part of the Japanese garden today. It is this combination of resolute determination to retain the ancient, mixed with an almost fanatic desire to borrow from the best of the new, that marks modern Japan, and especially modern Japanese gardens.

This tendency to bridge past and present can be seen in the minimalist rock creations of Isamu Noguchi's garden design for an ikebana school in Tokyo, a radical rendering of the dry-landscape motif. Likewise, Shinto myths and Buddhist enigmas mix with modern images in a Tokyo ward office, as their themes are played out in gold-leafed abstractions. The melding of the old and new can also be felt in the almost organic effect of a modern stone garden located under a busy highway in Tokyo, where what might be a serpent (or could it be a dragon?) writhes beneath a surface of granite slabs. To the Western eye, these examples might be seen as a departure from the disciplines of the past, but to the Japanese, they are merely part of the continuum.

That continuum was profoundly interrupted when war altered the complexion of the country. The fact that the ancient gardens of Kyoto were spared during World War II placed them in a sort of sacred trust. In Tokyo, a city forced to rebuild and reinvent itself after the war, gardens are more likely to break with traditional conventions, but never without consideration of the original design sources. Tradition, therefore, serves not to dictate, but to guide and to inspire bursts of creativity.

That first act of garden making, the tradition of marking off sacred ground—be it a single stone, a mountain, or a clearing in the woods—continues. These tributes to the power of nature still exist. A single vertical stone rising up out of a field, identified only by a simple rope, stands testament to the presence of the gods, while a farmer intently works the land around it, oblivious and yet sublimely aware of its existence. Certainly in their shrines and temples, in the lyrical countryside, and in the gray faces of their cities as well, the Japanese remain fervently attached to their gardens in all their glorious manifestations.

The portfolio of photographs included in this book was compiled over the course of a year, tracing the elements of the garden throughout four seasons. Each season revealed more of the gardens' wonders. In no month were we ever disappointed because the annuals had just withered, or because winter had stolen a garden's color. Instead, each season held more surprises.

No matter what the season, the familiar elements were there: the stones that have stood through centuries of turmoil, the ponds that have reflected Japan's rising sun since shoguns ruled, the sand and gravel that still ripple like waves on an ageless sea, the mosses, the noble pines, the bamboo that has swayed with a succession of changing winds. And always the intimate, yet vast, open, yet contained space, articulate in its silence.

We present these elements in unison, each contributing its part to the harmony of the garden.

A virtuous man when alone
loves the quiet of the mountains;
A wise man when in nature
enjoys the purity of the water.
One mustn't be suspicious of the fool
who takes pleasure in the
mountains and the streams,
But rather measure how well
he sharpens his spirit by them.
—MUSO SOSEKI

*Traditional architecture, as in
this tea house at Ritsurin-en, frames
the outside through sliding doors,
translucent walls, and wide
verandas.*

S T O N E

Lo, the stone of garden!
A glance of dignity
Even as of man
Who did put it there!
—MINAMOTO-NO-TOSHIYORI

Stone is truly the foundation of a Japanese garden, as well as its soul. Originally believed to harbor the gods, stones continue to be revered, if not as deities, then as personifications of the natural world.

Stones have been a part of gardening tradition ever since the ancients wrapped sacred ropes around them to designate the presence of a spirit. Since the twelfth century, garden designers were referred to as "stone-setting priests." So prized were certain stones in the feudal era that special privileges were granted by lords and shoguns to those who found particularly rare or unusual ones. Court nobles and commoners alike would flock into the mountains to search for stones with the extraordinary characteristics that imbued them with such worth.

Even today, garden stones can command hundreds of thousands of dollars. Professional "stone hunters" scour the countryside looking for specimens—so much so that certain areas have been placed off limits to stone gatherers. Stones are sold in rock nurseries, where they are displayed in settings as close to the stones' natural environs as possible. One such "store" in Kyoto seems to be a garden in itself, with all sizes and shapes of stones displayed among stone washbasins and lanterns. At a rock nursery in Gifu, a storehouse for particularly prized examples, it takes a full morning's work and a crane to move one stone that costs over $350,000.

Stones speak of the ages to the Japanese. Every crag, every edge worn to a smooth patina is evocative of the past. This quality, called *sabi*, gives a stone depth and power. The more subtle a stone's lines, the more it adds to a garden. Stones, with proper placement, can instantly add layers of age to a new garden.

A gardener chooses stones not only for their shape and color, but also for their personality. In accomplished hands, stones can suggest mountains, waterfalls, rushing rivers, or murmuring streams. Stones can be used to depict literal scenes from nature, art, or literature, but part of their attraction also lies in their ability to suggest and imply. A single stone may comprise an entire garden, while an assortment of stones—in groupings laid out in a dry landscape (*karesansui*)—can suggest animals, islands, or mountains.

The placement of rocks in a Japanese garden often looks random, even chaotic to the untrained eye. But this, like so much else within the garden, can at first be deceptive. Everything in a Japanese garden is highly choreographed. While the primary goal is to achieve

Unusual natural phenomena, such as this vermilion stone set in its own gravel garden near the priests' reception halls at Ise, were believed by early Shinto followers to harbor deities.

harmony within the garden, harmony does not necessarily mean symmetry. In fact, rough-hewn edges, odd numbers, and varying sizes and shapes enhance the garden's *sabi*.

The rules regarding placement have developed over the centuries and adapted to fit changing tastes, religious influences, and settings, but they were first codified in the *Sakuteiki*, an eleventh-century treatise on gardening. Many of the requirements set forth in *Sakuteiki* were based on Chinese geomantic laws that combined practical considerations such as hygiene and climate with more spiritual concerns surrounding the optimum flow of positive energy within a space. As a result, many gardening taboos are listed in the manuscript:

Sandals await guests on the kutsunugi-ishi *(shoe-removing stone) at the Yoshikawa ryokan (inn)*.

*There are instances where a stone originally found in the mountain or on the riverside certainly turns into a demon stone (*ishigami*) when it is moved and given the opportunity of assuming the pose of the demon stone, bringing a curse to people who, thereby, are obliged to leave the place soon.*

While garden designers still avoid improper placement of stones, they are more concerned with aesthetic considerations than with raising the ire of the spirit world.

Stones are said to have six faces, each with its own name. Careful attention is paid to the face a stone turns toward the viewer. The "root" of the stone is always set in the ground, to varying depths, depending upon the look the designer wants to achieve. In order to locate the optimum position for the stone, aside from the geomantic rules, the Japanese refer to *ishigokoro*, the "mind of the stone." The author of *Sakuteiki* frequently mentions this

principle of "following the request of the stone." The first rule in following a stone's directives is to listen: treated with proper concentration and respect, a stone will reveal where it should be placed.

One stone in the wrong place can sway the balance of the entire garden. This kind of balance is also addressed in *Sakuteiki*:

For the "running away" stones there are the "chasing" stones, for the leaning stone there is the supporting stone, for the trampling stone there is the trampled stone, for the looking-up stone there is the looking-down stone, and for the upright stone there is the lying stone.

Even the most seemingly random collections of stones are based on definite groupings. For example, often what appears to be a single stone is actually part of a triad, with the two other stones submerged or hidden from view.

Form is critical to stone placement, but so is function. Some stones are purely ornamental, serving an aesthetic purpose; others have prescribed uses. The *kutsunugi-ishi* (shoe-removing stone) is the flat stone seen outside of traditional Japanese homes, inns, and especially tea houses. Here, shoes are taken off and turned back towards the garden to be ready when their wearer leaves. Each *kutsunugi-ishi* is preceded by two "companion" stones that are considered separate from the path leading to them.

Many of the uses for stone stem from the tea ceremony. Because of the ceremony's links with Zen Buddhism, which stresses purity and lack of ornamentation, stone was the perfect element to embody these values.

The stone path became an integral part of the ceremony.

(Above and facing) Stepping stones are intrinsic to stroll gardens such as Koraku-en in Okayama. Their irregular placement slows the visitor's pace, directing his attention toward the designer's intended views.

The path of irregularly shaped stones approaching the inner garden was designed to ensure that visitors would arrive for the ceremony in the proper frame of mind. As the popularity of the tea garden grew— as even private courtyard gardens without tea houses began to incorporate many of their elements—the patterns of stepping stones became stylized. Some represent flying geese in formation (*ganko*) or the footprints of a Japanese sea bird called the plover (*chidori*), while other, more random placements were thought of as fields of fallen flowers (*rakka*). Occasionally, a millstone or foundation stone from an old building might be placed in the path, evocative of the passage of time. Small stones, known as "throwaway" stones (*sute-ishi*), are used to balance spots where the stepping stones lack harmony. They are never walked on.

The tea ceremony also brought stone lanterns and washbasins into gardens. Each lantern has its own style, for example, the *tachi-gata*, perched on pedestals, or the *ikekomi-gata*, with their bases planted firmly in the ground. They might be tiny (*oki-gata*), a flickering illumination at the edge of a pond, or massive, dominating a landscape. Some are placed on three legs; others are balanced on two. Some lanterns have umbrellalike tops that earn them the name of *yukimi* (snow-viewing lantern), because of the dancing shadows their light casts on freshly fallen snow.

Lanterns often illuminate a washbasin. Standing just to the side of the basin, the lantern would be lit when guests arrived for the tea ceremony at night. The basin, too, would be carved of stone, serving as both a literal and figurative washing place. Guests are expected to cleanse their hands, mouth, and mind of the residue of the outside world. These basins, like lanterns, are made in numerous styles.

Stone contributes to the ageless quality of a Japanese garden. Once properly placed, a stone can stand for centuries, changing only as lichens or moss subtly shade it. Its effectiveness is not altered with the seasons; its character is only enhanced by rain or snow.

If one sits on the veranda of Ryoan-ji in the early hours, before busloads of schoolchildren descend and taped exhortations on how to appreciate the garden crackle from loudspeakers, it is possible to hear the requests of the stones, to learn something of their minds. In the silence, broken only by the sounds of gravel being raked, the stones start to tell their stories. One need not ascribe to Shinto or Buddhist beliefs to appreciate the tales they share.

Stones and blossoming azaleas float in the midst of concentric ripples of sand, mimicking the islands in the pond beyond the Amida Hall at Byodo-in.

*Viewed from Otakamori,
the pine islands of
Matsushima Bay, one of
Japan's "Three Famous
Views," have inspired
poets and gardeners
alike.*

*This contemporary
garden in the local
government office of
Tokyo's Azabu district
features a granite sea
studded with gilded
rock islands.*

At Ritsurin-en, an eighteenth-century stroll garden, three rounded stones direct the eye from the shoreline to a graceful bridge arching over the water.

*A stone basin where guests
may cleanse their hands
and mouths is flanked by
a carved lantern at the
Yabunouchi Tea School
in Kyoto.*

Stone islands in this stream flowing through a pavilion in Koraku-en inspired Edo-era lords and ladies, who spent languid days composing verses and sipping sake from cups floating downstream.

S A N D & G R A V E L

At last! In sunshine

sparrows

are bathing in sand,

fluffing their feathers.

—ONITSURA

Perhaps no other garden element is more evocative than gravel. It has the timeless qualities of stone, and yet is fluid and mutable. In that sense, it satisfies the Japanese reverence for the permanence of the past as well as the Zen doctrine of the changeability of life. Its use in gardens stems from primitive times, when early Shinto followers spread white gravel in sacred groves (*niwa*) to attract the spirits of nature. The grounds of Ise's inner shrine, built in the third century, are covered in this kind of gravel, creating a vast sea with subtle shadings and variations.

This model became the prototype for all Shinto shrines; today, small whitish gray pebbles have replaced the gravel used in the early *niwa*.

The courtyards of the imperial palaces were patterned after the early shrines, incorporating vast gravel tracts that formed the courtyards of their residences. From the verandas of the *shinden* halls, nobles looked out upon sweeps of gravel and beyond toward elaborate renderings of lakes dotted with islands and artificially constructed hills and streams. The gravel provided an austere complement to the more ornamental hill-and-island gardens.

Gravel's suggestive qualities, and the ease with which its shapes and shadings change, made it perfectly suited to the *karesansui* (dry garden) landscape that was popularized during the Muromachi period. Gravel in a dry landscape most often represents water: a serene sea, a gushing torrent of rapids, a trickle

of water from a shallow stream.

At Ryoan-ji, perhaps the most well-known dry landscape in the world, gravel plays a huge role in the garden's primary function: meditation. The vast, monochromatic swirls of the garden, broken by fifteen horizontal and vertical stones, stimulate the imaginations not only of those who observe it from the veranda, but also of those who tend it.

Because gravel is so fluid and requires constant maintenance, Zen Buddhist practice incorporated the raking of it into meditation rituals as a form of spiritual discipline. Patterns that were etched hundreds of years ago are still raked with unceasing regularity. It is believed that if total concentration is given to the task, flashes of enlightenment (*satori*) can be achieved. The fact that a heavy downpour can obliterate all those hours of work coincides with Zen thought. In Zen, all that matters is the moment—not what went yesterday and not what will come tomorrow. Sands can blow and shift, ripples of gravel can be wiped smooth; a garden is always in a state of flux. In a sense, a garden dies and is reborn daily, part of the continual cycle of life. The scrape of a wooden rake across the gravel sea is a sign of this continuum.

Patterns of sand and gravel became stylized into distinct forms, each with its own name reminiscent of the way that water moves: large waves (*uneri*), scalloped waves (*katao-nami*), ripples (*sazanami*), parallel zigzag lines (*ajiro-nami*), and whirlpools (*uzumaki-mon*).

Thus, depending upon the

The province of meditative monks in the early morning and evening hours, Ryoan-ji is a requisite stop for busloads of students throughout the day.

The maintenance of the dry garden at Tentoku-en in Mount Koya affords ample opportunity for concentration on the wavelike patterns first traced by Zen priests hundreds of years ago.

pattern, motion can be introduced into a static landscape. Waves can be made to wash against ragged shores, a whirlpool to spin towards its center, and concentric ripples to spread as if a pebble has just been thrown into a pond. A pattern called "blue waves" (*seikaiha*) resembles a fish's scales, creating the effect of a fish darting beneath the surface of the water.

Not just any type of gravel or sand is used in gardens. Too fine a grain is easily blown away; too heavy or too dark a grain inhibits the fluidity of the medium. The type most preferred is weathered white or gray granite with a grain of about five millimeters in diameter. Kyoto's Shirakawa district provides an abundance of this type to supply the gardens there. Finer-grained sand is also used, but only in contained

spaces and in limited quantities.

The use of varying sizes of gravel accounts for much of the electric quality of Daisen-in at Daitoku-ji Complex in Kyoto. The froth from the rushing cascade tumbling into the sea is almost palpable. The currents of white and gray gravel seem to sweep the small boat in the pool beneath the waterfall south through the garden.

Although monochromatic tones are most frequently seen in dry landscapes, echoing Sung landscape paintings, gravel and sand of different colors are used as well. Subtlety is desired when working with gravel; subdued colors are thought to create the most dramatic effects. A chronicle from the Muromachi period called the *Ashikaga chiran-ki* notes that gravel in five colors was used at Kinkaku-ji, the residence of Ashikaga shogun Yoshimitsu. This bed of gravel between a stand of cherry trees and the structure was raked into a pattern intended to represent wavelets on the surface of the sea.

Another gravel sea at Ginkaku-ji, a temple-residence built in 1482 by Yoshimasa, grandson of Yoshimitsu, is more enigmatic. The "waters," known as Ginsadan (silver sand sea), have been raked in the same wavelike pattern since their addition to the garden during the Edo era,

and their designs create a spectacular sweep as their colors reflect the light and shadows of the sky. It is said that this garden is best viewed under a full moon rising to the east. The sand ripples with a silvery glint, and some say the Land of Happiness presents itself. The effect of moon viewing is further enhanced by a puzzling cone to the side of the gravel sea.

This type of cone is frequently seen in Japanese temple and shrine gardens, but it has no easy explanation. On first glance, this truncated cone of sand, kept flawlessly intact by constant leveling and shaping, suggests a miniature rendition of the sacred Mount Fuji, but there is no evidence that this was the idea behind the shape. What is more likely is that the cone evolved from the piles of gravel kept beside dry landscapes to replenish

the patterns after nobles walked across them or rain, wind, or snow erased them. The cone, however mundane its origins, seems to harmonize with the raked waves, especially under the full moon.

As with so many aspects of Japanese garden design, gravel often serves a practical purpose. It provides excellent drainage, and also helps in keeping feet from getting muddied. It can line a pathway through a stroll garden or be placed around the base of trees

to keep weeds from spreading. Gravel around a washbasin and at the base of a rain gutter helps with drainage.

Sand can be used to create an illusion of expansiveness in a garden. It is seen often in small courtyard gardens, which may consist of nothing more than an

To preserve the precision of the sand cone at Ginkaku-ji, gardeners plane the surface regularly with a wooden mason's trowel.

A gravel whirlpool swirls around the massive stone configurations of jagged islands and mountains that dominate the south garden at Tofuku-ji in Kyoto.

50

enclosure of a few square feet and a single stone on a bed of sand.

But it can also blanket vast spaces, its patterns conveying an assortment of abstract concepts. In a checkerboard pattern, such as the one at Tofuku-ji near Kyoto, the geometric regularity of the grid casts an almost hypnotic effect. It can be seen as a reference to the yin and yang of Chinese philosophy, a physical representation of the coexistence of opposites. This contrasting of elements is often seen in Japanese gardens. At Ginkaku-ji, for example, the sand and gravel sea acts as a counterpoint to a pictur- esque pond garden. The "sea" laps at the shores of the planted area, but is a distinct and separate part of the garden. In other gardens, stark sand is balanced by lush mosses nibbling at its edges.

The reflective properties of white sand or gravel draw light into the garden, brightening the *tsubo*

gardens set in passageways or inner courtyards. But a spread of gravel, like a pond, can also absorb darkness, casting a gray mood over a garden on a cloudy day.

In the traditional uses of sand or fine gravel, as in the courtyards of imperial residences, there is an air of formality. Because of the starkness of the medium, sand and gravel gardens create islands of serenity. They are at once plain canvases on which a designer chooses to express himself and blank maps that will lead a viewer wherever his thoughts and emotions dictate. But modern garden designers have made other uses of sand's characteristic adaptability. At the golf clubs near Tokyo, the titans of industry and the merely fanatic may wind up caught in a whimsical sand trap that has all the elements of a perfect Japanese garden.

A decorative stone lantern stands sentry amidst blue pines and gleaming white sand in the garden of the Adachi Museum.

*Raked gravel patterns on the
sand mounds at Honen-in in
Kyoto are changed by temple
priests to suit the season: a
maple-leaf design heralds fall.*

Rippled sand can be startlingly fluid and reflective, such as here at Zuiho-in in Kyoto, creating, in the words of poet Simpei Kusana, a "river where no water runs."

*The enigmatic gravel sea
and stone islands of Ryoan-ji
make it the archetype of Zen
gardens.*

54

Stone footpaths convey the mood of the garden, be it formal, semiformal, or informal—shin, gyo, or so. This gyo path leads to the tea house at the Adachi Museum in Yasugi.

*The precise placement of
pebbles and stones in a
manmade streambed creates
the illusion of the sound and
velocity of rushing water at
Shinyo-in in Kyoto.*

The kuzushi, *a path of irregular stones and pebbles edged by gravel, leads to the famous Ichi-riki tea house in Kyoto's Gion district, where geisha have entertained wealthy customers for over 300 years.*

W
A
T
E
R

A pool reflecting
White clouds…
Deep in a bamboo
Shadow, a fish stirs.
—SHURIN

Japan is an island country, surrounded by and dependent on the sea for its existence. Because no part of Japan is more than a few hours from the coast, the Japanese have a reverence and a fascination for the sea. That fact, combined with the religious connotations of water, make it a powerful symbol for the Japanese.

Religion played an early role in the connection of water and gardens. Shinto purification rites mandated the presence of water in shrine gardens. Buddhist imagery, with innumerable references to oceans, lakes, and ponds, influenced temple gardens. One of the earliest recorded gardens in Japan

was built in the island-pond motif seen repeatedly in Buddhist painting. The style became formalized in the Jodo gardens of the Amidist Buddhist sect.

T'ang and Sung landscape paintings, in which seascapes, rivers, and waterfalls are featured, inspired the Japanese to recreate the scenes depicted. Commerce with China and Korea spurred returning travelers to incorporate the best of the natural vistas they saw on their journeys into the gardens of their homes and temples. Renditions of Japan's "Three Famous Views"— Matsushima (Pine Islands) Bay, the craggy coastal cliffs of Shiogama, and the Amano-hashidate sandbar stretching across Miyazu Bay—are recurring themes in Japanese gardens.

When natural conditions did not offer water sources, the Japanese created them. If a design called for a pond, designers would dig one,

forming hills and islands with the turf they excavated. Reverent of nature, yet always ready to control it, the Japanese recognized that water needed to be contained and directed, but in subtle ways that disguised any artifice. Often ponds were carved in the pattern of a particularly significant character (*kanji*), such as the ones for "heart" (*shin-ji*) or "water" (*mizu*). Strictly

geometric forms were avoided.

Kyoto's location, surrounded by mountains, with ample rivers and underground springs, made bringing water into gardens an easy task—a fact that helped make the city a center for garden building. Water was channeled from natural springs into meandering, shallow streams. In the Heian period, water was generally drawn from the north side

of a building, its flow directed under the veranda of the main quarters, then under the other buildings, and off on a winding journey to end in a pond. Motion in water was aesthetically important, but it was also necessary to prevent stagnation.

The garden manual *Sakuteiki* explains the proper flow of water in

a stream, according to the laws of geomancy:

The most auspicious way is to let the stream start from the east side, come through under the building, and then flow toward the south-west direction. This is to conform to the principle of

This scene at the daimyo stroll garden Suizen-ji in Kumamoto, with Mount Fuji rendered in miniature, is a recreation of one of the fifty-three famous views along the Tokaido, Japan's most celebrated road.

washing out all kinds of evil spirits lurking in the way of the White Tiger (byakko) of the west side, with the water of the Blue Dragon (seiryu) of the east side. Then, it is said, the master of the house would be freed from epidemics and skin diseases, and enjoy good health, happiness and long life.

Water features in the gardens of feudal lords and courtiers were designed for recreation. Boating parties would cast off from the docks alongside pavilions and glide along the lake for cherry blossom and moon viewing, as well as fishing. Sometimes water would flow through one of the pavilions, channeled between the sides of a specially constructed veranda. At Koraku-en, guests were invited to lounge alongside this interior stream, sip sake out of tiny cups, and write poetry. Some nobles would challenge their guests to write poems as they floated sake cups on the stream through the pavilion. The objective was to complete a poem before the sake reached the author.

The soothing babble of water running through the poem-writing pavilion contrasted with the force of a spilling waterfall. *Sakuteiki* lists ten types of waterfalls, each emphasizing a different rock pattern to evoke different sounds and effects: facing-, one-way-, running-, leaping-, corner-, linen-, thread-, compound-, left-, and right-falling. The author of *Sakuteiki* also refers to the Buddhist symbolism of the waterfall:

Acala, the God (Fudo-myoo) [a Buddhist deity] avowed that any waterfall attaining a height of three feet represents his body. How much more so, then, if the fall reaches the height of four, five, or even ten or twenty feet! Well enough, such tall waterfalls always take the form of the Buddhistic trinity (sanzon), by which the two front stones on the right and the left represent the two Junior Attendants (doji) of the celestial family of Acala.

Each waterfall construction was based on this trinity format of a large "water-falling" stone flanked by two side stones. These manmade falls are still major focal points in gardens.

At the foot of the waterfall in the garden of Tenryu-ji is a large stone referred to as the Carp Stone. This stone recalls the Chinese legend of the noble carp who fought its way up a massive waterfall, doggedly struggling through the rapids in order to reach the top and be transformed into a dragon, the Chinese symbol for emperor. Thus the carp represents perseverance and determination. The vermilion shades of these shimmering fish bring living color to a garden, and

*Rain awakens the greens of the
garden, enriching the varied hues
of moss at Saiho-ji (above) and
polishing the leaves of a lily
(facing).*

The iris-edged yatsuhashi *(eight-fold bridge) at Koraku-en straddles a stream in an allusion to* The Tales of Ise. *Views from the bridge are directed by its angles.*

the varying hues of the fish add dimension to the water. The bright oranges, golds, and whites, and especially the celebratory reds, flash with the whisk of a tail as the carp dart beneath lotus blossoms or water lilies floating on the surface.

Water is especially apparent in the tea garden. Tea masters will often sprinkle water on the moss-covered rocks leading to the tea house to enhance the color and bring out the patina of the stone. Guests stop and wash their hands at a stone washbasin, which might be fed by a spring. The gentle gurgle of water rushing over the side of the basin helps guests leave the cacophony of the outside world behind. Dipping a bamboo ladle into the basin and sipping the fresh water cools a visitor and symbolically purifies his mouth as well. The clear clack of a bamboo *shishi-odoshi* against a stone after it empties of the water it has collected may frighten animals away from eating moss and cultivated vegetables, but it also gives a gentle punctuation to the solitude of the garden.

Streams in stroll gardens provide a meandering course to follow through the grounds. Pathways and bridges carry visitors along and over these waterways. A zigzagging, eight-planked bridge in Koraku-en in Okayama is angled to guarantee that guests won't hurry over a crystalline stream and miss the views. Its pattern is borrowed from a ninth-century poem by an exiled courtier, who crossed such a bridge as he was heading for the remote provinces. In the poem, he writes of stopping at each of the angles of the bridge to pause and reflect upon all that he was leaving behind.

In addition to manipulating water into artificial ponds and streams, the Japanese also take advantage of natural sources of water. Long chains of tiny loops extend from eaves in lieu of gutters, drawing rainwater down an intricate path along the chain. The effect is a soft trickle, rather than a gushing wash of rainwater, as it gently spills onto a cluster of water-polished drainage stones.

Gardens look their best in the rain; moisture brings out the texture of the monochromatic dry landscapes and the greens of the flora. Saiho-ji, Kyoto's "Moss Temple," comes to life in the rain, as the more than one hundred varieties of emerald moss shimmer and undulate over roots and stones.

Through reflections in water, the sky, the trees, or the mountains in the background of a garden are embraced into the garden confines. Shugakuin in Kyoto artfully captures this extra dimension. Emperor Gomizuno designed this Edo-era garden for himself and incorporated the natural vistas beyond the site into his plan. The lake absorbs the colors of the sky, changing the mood of the garden with the time of day or season. On a gray or snowy day, the reflections on the lake transform Shugakuin into a Sung monochrome; during a summer sunset, a golden sun burns a hole through the surface of the water; in autumn, the blaze of color from surrounding maples dapples the lake; and in spring, the water is as fresh as the new blossoms surrounding it.

The carp's propitious golden red color and hardiness make it a frequent addition to a garden pond.

A flash of living color, carp beneath a pond's surface add subtle adornment to the Adachi Museum garden.

Each season, even winter, adds its own flourishes to a garden. The first snowfall transforms the pond-and-island garden of Motsu-ji in Hiraizumi into a Sung monochrome.

In Gumna prefecture, the manmade pools
into which pour the thermal springs of
Takaragawa onsen were designed to
resemble natural rock outcroppings
and pools.

*Dubbed a "deer scare"
because of the clacking
sound it makes, a
bamboo* shishi-odoshi
*fills with water and
empties into a basin
or stream.*

*Swaying reeds rustle
and whisper along the
pond edge at Shisendo
in Kyoto.*

The seas that surround Japan are rife with sacred significance. A Shinto torii sits atop the largest of the Meoto-Iwa (Wedded Rocks) of Futamigaura near Ise, marking the stones as a shrine dedicated to Izanagi and Isanami, the legendary creators of Japan.

Even in the starkest and most
compact of landscapes composed
of rock and gravel, the Japanese
gardener often includes a
representation of a pond,
such as this one at Zuiho-in.

75

Vibrant maple foliage is reflected in the steaming pools of Takaragawa onsen, where a bather douses himself in thermal waters channeled from the springs through a bamboo pipe.

F
L
O
R
A

The well-trod path
Is covered with fallen leaves
Sweep them aside
To view the footprints
   of the Sun Goddess.
—NINOMIYA

If a visitor finds a few tiny, crimson maple leaves along a path in a Japanese tea garden in October, it is not by accident. The tea master most probably left them there as he was sweeping to remind his guests of the fleeting quality of time.

Living things throughout their growth cycles from full-bloom to bare branches distinguish Japanese gardens, unlike Western gardens, so independent of seasonal vagaries. The plants in a garden provide forever changing, and forever fascinating, marvels.

Plants are not grown in a Japanese garden for cultivation, as they are in Western gardens. The flowers grown there are not for picking, nor is the fruit for eating.

Rather, all plants are considered elements of design, just as are stone and gravel.

Choosing the plants for a Japanese garden is a matter of tradition, taste, and technique. Dating back to the origins of Shinto, trees have always held mystical significance. Divine spirits are believed to dwell in them, just as they are believed to live in stones or mountains. Gautama Buddha was said to have reached enlightenment while sitting under a tree. Certain trees are especially revered: the pine for its durability and longevity; the cherry for its blossoms and hard wood; and the plum, a Chinese import, for its hardiness.

The very first gardens were devoid of vegetation. But as Buddhist imagery began to inspire garden builders, the plants associated with the various deities of that faith found their way into gardens. The lotus is foremost of these. Symbolic of the Buddha, it is often seen in the ponds of Jodo gardens.

As the garden grew into an idealization of a natural landscape, trees and grasses that suggested windswept shorelines were added. Pine trees were particularly suited to this, since their branches are relatively easy to train into shapes evoking the effects of age and weather. Elaborate pruning techniques were used to achieve these results: needles were handpicked from branches to open up views beyond the tree, alternating branches were sheared from the trunk to give a leaner look to the tree, and trunks were tied and bound to groom them into the gnarls and bends of a centuries-old pine. Often the branches need the support of wooden crutches as they are being trained to extend out over ponds or islands.

The same intricate, time-consuming, and labor-intensive techniques are still used in gardens today. Electric mowers and clippers are almost never seen. Gardeners still spend hours hunched over

Tufted moss engulfs the gnarled
roots of a spreading maple at
Saiho-ji, where the optimum
conditions of shade, humidity,
and moist clay soil cause moss
varieties to proliferate.

79

The tying of yukizuri (rice-fiber ropes) to protect pine branches from breaking under the weight of snow is an annual feat performed at Kenroku-en in Kanazawa.

small plots, painstakingly picking pine needles and twigs from the ground cover. The manual trimming of trees is taken to its most extreme in the art of bonsai. In bonsai, actual trees, usually seedlings, are transferred to earthenware pots and tied, twisted, wrapped, and clipped on an almost daily basis, in order to stunt growth. This art became prevalent as room for gardens grew scarcer.

The most popular plants in Japanese gardens are those indigenous to the area. These are called *niwaki*; all others are referred to as *zoki*. Besides the pine, cherry, and plum trees, among those most often seen are the cryptomeria cedar, Japanese cypress, Chinese black pine, pomegranate, oak, azalea, ilex, and Japanese maple.

A tree is usually a focal point of the garden, with other plants included as accents. Growth is constantly checked to preserve the overall design. That explains why

bamboo is used with restraint, despite its grace and hardiness. Fifteen varieties can be found in Japan, but the giant grass grows so well that, once its lateral root systems take hold, it will literally consume a garden.

On one hand, Japanese gardens are silent testimony to continuity and stability; on the other, each season gives a garden a new look. Snow, rain, early summer's golden greens, late summer's umber shades, and autumn color are all special effects in a gardener's repertoire.

In celebration of the New Year, the "Three Friends of Winter," the pine, bamboo, and plum, are celebrated in decorative displays throughout Japan. These hardy trees signal that life will stir again after the winter's cold. But even the most durable of trees often cannot survive a harsh winter without help from man. In the snow country of northern Japan, the pine boughs in the feudal stroll garden, Kenroku-en,

are individually tied with rice-fiber ropes suspended from the tops of the trees in order to support the branches under the weight of wet snows. Tropical cycads are wrapped in straw overcoats to protect them from cold winds.

Spring is the time that the often somber gardens go wild with a profusion of blossoms. The cherry tree, patron of scholars and literary men, drops little petals of pink and white, while factory workers and housewives, "salary-men" and students take a break from their routine and troop out to the parks and gardens to take in the blossoms.

In spring, azaleas are allowed to blossom in a blaze of color; they are kept closely pruned the rest of the year. The shapes of these shrubs enhance and complement the gardens of Suizen-ji, a daimyo stroll garden.

Fallen leaves in autumn (above) are a reminder of the transience of the seasons and the passage of time. This cyclical theme is recurrent in Japanese gardens, so many of which have evolved through centuries of growth and decay. Moss, seen at Saiho-ji (facing), adds an aura of age to a garden.

These cherry-blossom-appreciation picnics (*hanami*) have been held since the eighth century, when nobles would host huge flower-viewing parties and mark the occasions by composing haiku. The samurai held that the cherry was the soul of *bushido* (chivalry) and that *bushido* was the soul of Japan. The cherry's fleeting blooms reminded the samurai that their glory days as warriors could end just as

abruptly as the cherry blossoms fall to the ground.

Azaleas take over later in the spring. Green throughout most of the year, they blossom in riotous pinks, magentas, and reds. Azaleas are prized because they take discipline well; they are clipped and trained into hedges to guide a visitor's approach or direct his eyes to a particular view, and occasion-ally become a garden in themselves, as at Daichi-ji. Through artful shearing, the plant becomes not just topiary, but organic sculpture. As the wind blows or the blossoms open or fall, the entire scene changes.

The iris arrive in the summer, accompanied by an assortment of literary references from *The Tale of Genji* and other Japanese classics. Often seen growing alongside ponds or streams, the iris create borders of color.

If spring announces the beginning of a life cycle, then autumn, with ripe russets and golds, is a harbinger

of its final days. The spectacle of the red maples in the hills outside Kyoto, or along the mountains near the Takaragawa onsen, where the fall mist rises up out of thermal springs like a sheer veil over the colors of the trees, is exhilarating and yet melancholy.

The poet Basho writes of the season and his travels to a temple garden and a hot spring:

Whiter far
Than the white rocks
Of the Rock Temple
The autumn wind blows.

Bathed in such comfort
In the balmy spring of Yamanaka,
I can do without plucking
Life-preserving chrysanthemums.

Chrysanthemum cultivation is practically a cult in Japan. The crest of the imperial family since the Meiji era and their symbol since long before that, the chrysanthemum is linked to the sun goddess and the rising sun of Japan. In fact, the pre-World War II version of the Japanese flag featured a sixteen-petaled chrysanthemum with a central disk.

Although the plant is not seen in tea or meditation gardens, in the autumn it's hard to miss a display of chrysanthemums. Cultivated to perfection in pots, in dramatic cascades, and even as period costumes on mannequins, chrysan-themums dominate during fall.

Though the garden offers spots of color throughout the year, the most prominent tone, besides the grays of the rocks and stones, is green. Moss, seen sneaking up on stones and edging into gravel seas, is ubiqui-tous, and is particularly suited to Japan's humid, temperate climate.

Over a hundred varieties of moss practically pave Saiho-ji, the garden popularly known as Kokedera. While not an original feature of the garden, the moss through the years eventually carpeted the grounds, creating a velvety floor for this

enchanted forest. The mosses were such an attraction that the garden had to be closed to the public not long ago; fumes from the tour buses toting tourists to Saiho-ji were damaging the delicate plants. Now admittance is by special permission only.

A reverence for the natural world is indigenous to Japan; throughout the Japanese garden is a sense of eternity. As *Sakuteiki*'s author writes: "Trees really embellish the world, making it comparable to the heavenly world." It's hard not to imagine that the living things in a

garden are a bridge between this world and whatever lies beyond.

Not yet having become a Buddha,
This ancient pine tree,
Idly dreaming.
— ISSA

The pine tree, considered sacred by the ancients, is hand-pruned at Ritsurin-en into shapes that recall trees along windswept coasts.

At Sanzen-in in Kyoto,
fallen maple leaves on
a blanket of sukigoke
moss serve as reminders
of the cycles of nature.

June brings the irises to Kenroku-en. The Japanese iris is popular among practitioners of ikebana, the art of flower arrangement, and is a frequent motif on lacquerware.

*The Japanese skill and
penchant for miniaturization
reaches its zenith in the art of
bonsai, practiced by more
than thirty artists in the
town of Omiya.*

*A bird's-eye view of Tokyo
reveals patches of green—
here, the Meiji shrine, a
recent garden (1915–
1920) reminiscent of
Western parks—amidst
the gray concrete.*

Pine boughs, pruned for horizontal growth, are supported by wooden crutches at Koishikawa Koraku-en, near Iidabashi in Tokyo.

Twisted into contortions, the trunk of this pine tree in a Kyoto suburb has been trained to follow the whims of the gardener who has weighted its branches.

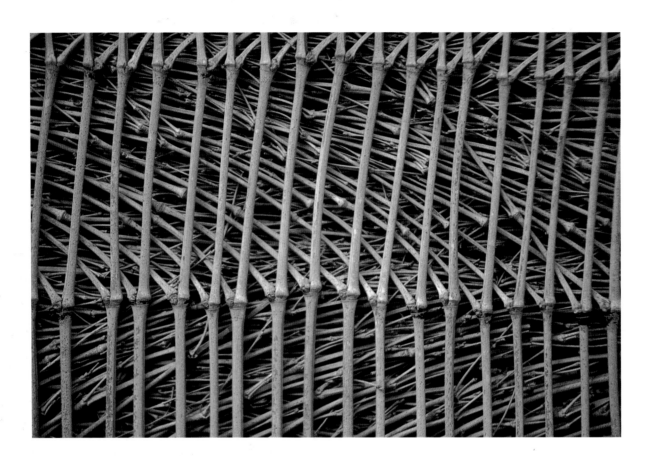

Boundaries in Japanese gardens are more often suggested than defined. Latticed bamboo fences mark borders, allowing light and sound to pass through this fence at Shisendo.

A stand of swaying bamboo at Saiho-ji creates a natural fence. Rustling stalks add the dimension of sound to the garden's atmosphere.

In a typically Japanese landscape at Saiho-ji, trees and plants meld in subtle harmony with the other elements of the garden.

*A tree's shadow casts
the poetry of light and
dark shapes on a field of
white gravel at
Shisendo.*

*A hint of the space
beyond, a branch peeks
through an opening in an
earthen garden wall in
Kyoto's Gion district.*

SPACE

Under the temple eaves
  Gold fades...
Through budding leaves
  We look toward the past.
—CHORA

Often what is *not* seen in a Japanese garden speaks most eloquently. Just as in Chinese landscape painting, where empty space links the heavens and the earth, space in the Japanese garden unites its often disparate parts, creating a total composition. To the Japanese aesthetic, empty spaces are not merely voids waiting to be filled; they are garden elements in themselves, tools to be utilized and mastered.

The irony of modern Japanese garden design is that there is a distinct lack of space in that country. In Japan, 120 million people live in an area not much larger than the state of California. And yet, despite the population density and the crowded cities and highways, nowhere is nature revered and celebrated more heartily. Homes and offices, no matter how crowded their interior spaces, make room for a garden—in a corner, along a corridor, at the end of a hallway, or on a rooftop.

During the classical Heian period, court nobles and military regents could command vast tracts for their pleasure gardens. But as land became scarcer and the population grew, gardens diminished in size. This dimunition also corresponded to the growing impact of Zen Buddhism. Zen practice emphasized restraint and rejected lavish displays of opulence, setting the stage for the creation of worlds in miniature and eventually, worlds in the abstract.

Zen monks introduced concepts of their philosophy into their garden designs, and transformed the garden from a place for amusement and relaxation to a spot for solitude and contemplation. Skilled at manipulating spatial proportions, Zen garden designers left a legacy of reductivism for modern gardening. By juggling perspectives, the Zen garden masters could use space as a means of enlarging or shrinking an area, making a distant mountain seem near or a small pond seem enormous.

Dry-landscape gardens like Kyoto's Ryoan-ji and Daisen-in play with our sense of size and scale. Ryoan-ji is at first sight an apparently static composition of fifteen stones in three groupings. But as the eye travels across the landscape, the mind can sense motion. The scene may depict, as some scholars have said, a tiger and her cubs crossing a river, but the real meaning lies in the imagination of the beholder.

Daisen-in, while a literal interpretation of a painting, nevertheless offers viewers a confounding scale. In photographs, it appears to be an almost life-size landscape with waterfall and river. The falling cascade seems powerful,

The garden changes with the viewer's perspective. Glimpsed from behind shoji, the tea garden at the Adachi Museum is both hidden and revealed.

Architecture adds to the spatial qualities of the garden: lines of the veranda, post, and sliding walls of a tea house frame an intimate corner of Ritsurin-en.

humbling the small boat at its base. But the true size of the garden is startling. Only twelve feet deep, this garden is truly a landscape in miniature. The illusion is effected by staggering the elements of the garden: a small, yet dynamic cascade in the rear, connoting distance, balanced with a boat and bridge closer to the foreground,

creating the illusion of proximity and size. Proportionately, the boat is larger than the falls, but its location in the landscape dwarfs it in relationship to the waterfall. The result is to remind the viewer of how easily the forces of nature overwhelm man.

The Japanese have developed an adeptness with visual tricks to create such desired illusions. This is one of

the many ways that a Japanese garden differs from a Western one. While nature is invited into the garden, it is not allowed a free hand. And yet, a garden should never give away its secret: the mark of the gardener and his devices should never be apparent. The overall effect should always be as true to nature as possible, and often, an idealization of what nature ought to be. A

gardener may include a horizontal line—be it an earthen wall, a stretch of raked gravel, or a hedge—to extend or contract a space or to direct the eye along a horizontal plane, but the conscious mind will not be aware of his method. He might set three stones across a small brook to create a floating bridge, but the observer will never see the submerged base stones that support it.

Japanese gardens, while they are contained, are never entirely sealed off from the world beyond them. A fence, a wall, or a hedge acts more as a link between the garden and what lies outside. As a result, surrounding scenery becomes a part of the garden. This concept of "borrowed scenery" (*shakkei*) is beautifully illustrated at the Adachi Museum in Yasugi. From a vantage point inside the museum, looking out into the garden designed by Kinsaku Nakane, it seems to embrace an entire panorama, including the sky, a distant waterfall, and mountains off toward the horizon, all reflected in the waters of the pond. What is not seen is the highway that snakes its way behind the stand of trees marking the literal confines of the garden. The designer succeeds in enlarging the space of the garden, while eliminating from view what would have been a jarring intrusion of cars and trucks. When a gardener selects a site,

after he has determined that the natural conditions there are appropriate to his designs, he then takes into consideration the elements beyond the confines of the space. In incorporating borrowed scenery, gardeners work on three planes. The first is the foreground within the garden; the last is the distant landscape. In between is the focal line that divides and defines the view between near and far. Often it is a stand of trees or hedges, pruned so that only their leafy top sections remain, leaving their trunks to provide a bare frame for the picture.

Framing is essential to Japanese garden design and appreciation. Directed views predominate—be they glanced through an opening in an azalea hedge or gazed at between the perpendicular lines of rice-paper shoji screens. Designers intend observers to see the gardens at

specific angles and through calculated approaches. In essence, the gardener defines the space of the garden for the viewer. It is not unheard of for designers to mark spots on stones, as at the Adachi Museum, to indicate to visitors the optimum spot for viewing. Rather than inhibiting the imagination, the technique of prescribed viewing merely ensures that the details of the garden will not be missed.

Framing a view also tames a massive panorama, reducing it to a scale that is more pleasing than if it were seen in its entirety. Some vistas are too overwhelming to be appreciated without boundaries; the mind tends to travel over them searching for some small element to grasp. Framing provides an intimacy, such as the view of the garden at Kyoto's Shisendo through the round second-story window

designed for moon viewing. Using a device entirely appropriate to an art museum, one section of the garden at the Adachi Museum is permanently showcased in a picture frame hung around a window, to be viewed from inside the building as living art.

The juxtaposition of elements in a garden can create a variety of sensations, but perhaps the most powerful is that felt when encountering a completely empty space enclosed by an earthen wall or bamboo fence—the garden as total abstraction. Open, flat spaces filled only with dry, raked gravel are still the essence of garden making in Japan. To experience the mental journey that occurs when absorbing the motion inherent in the static patterns is to know something of a garden's most important secret—the achievement of *ma*—the stimulation of all the senses in time and space.

Once free of distractions, all of the senses can be tuned. Even the sounds of the garden begin to reveal themselves: a monk's chanting, the clack of a *shishi-odoshi* as it empties of water and hits its base rock, a temple gong, the rustle of a stand of bamboo swaying in the breeze. Soon, the blank space becomes full. For even when a garden is at its most minimal—nothing but a bare stretch of raked sand—it is often at its most provocative. As Zen scholars understood, the mind needs only the barest hints before it can be catapulted on a fascinating journey.

Parallel lines and a round moon-viewing window capture outside spaces at Shisendo (facing). An abstract gravel checkerboard at Tofuku-ji (above) suggests a grid of rice paddies.

Framed and viewed from within the Adachi Museum as a masterpiece of living art, this scene encompasses the "borrowed" mountains silhouetted against a distant horizon.

INDEX OF GARDENS

SUFFIXES

Many garden names contain the suffixes whose meanings are here listed:

-en = garden
-gu = shrine
-in = temple
-ji = subtemple

BIBLIOGRAPHY

THE GARDENS OF JAPAN, Teiji Itoh, Tokyo: Kodansha International, 1982.

GATEWAY TO JAPAN, June Kinoshita and Nicholas Palevsky, Tokyo: Kodansha International, 1990.

A GUIDE TO THE GARDENS OF KYOTO, Ron Herman and Marc Treib, Tokyo: Shufunotomo Co., Ltd., 1980.

JAPAN: A HISTORY IN ART, Bradley Smith, New York: Doubleday & Co., Inc., 1964.

JAPAN: THE NEW OFFICIAL GUIDE, compiled by the Japan National Tourist Organization, Japan: Japan Travel Bureau Inc., 1975.

THE JAPANESE COURTYARD GARDEN: LANDSCAPES FOR SMALL SPACES, Kanto Shigemori, New York: John Weatherhill, Inc., 1981.

JAPANESE COURTYARD GARDENS, Haruzo Ohashi, Tokyo: Graphic-sha Publishing Co., Ltd., 1988.

THE JAPANESE GARDEN: ISLANDS OF SERENITY, Haruzo Ohashi, Tokyo: Graphic-sha Publishing Co., Ltd., 1986.

A JAPANESE TOUCH FOR YOUR GARDEN, David H. Engel, Masanobu Kudo, and Kiyoshi Seika, Tokyo: Kodansha International, 1980.

KYOTO GARDENS, Kinsaku Nakane, Osaka: Hoikusha Publishing Co., Ltd., 1965.

SAKUTEIKI: THE BOOK OF GARDEN, Tachibana-no-Toshitsuna, translated by Shigemaru Shimoyama, Tokyo: Town and City Planners, Inc., 1985

THE WORLD OF THE JAPANESE GARDEN: FROM CHINESE ORIGINS TO MODERN LANDSCAPE ART, Loraine Kuck, New York: John Weatherhill, Inc., 1968.

POETRY SELECTIONS

PAINTED FANS OF JAPAN: 15 NOH DRAMA MASTERPIECES, edited by Reiko Chiba; Rutland, Vermont and Tokyo: Charles E. Tuttle Company, 1962, 1977.

THE NARROW ROAD TO THE DEEP NORTH, Matsuo Basho, translated by Nobuyuji Yuasa, London: Penguin Books, 1966.

HAIKU HARVEST, translation by Harry Behn and Peter Beilenson, Mount Vernon, New York: The Peter Pauper Press, 1962.

This book is dedicated

to the memory of my father,

Susumu Yamashita, who

shared with us his love

of the garden.

ACKNOWLEDGMENTS

Special thanks to the National Geographic Society, the National Gallery of Art, and to the following people, without whom this book would not have been possible: Tom Kennedy, Kent Kobersteen, Bill Garrett, Tom Smith, Kate Glassner, Susan Welchman, Bob Madden, Kunio Kadowaki, Robert Kirschenbaum, and Marcy Posner.

Michael S. Yamashita